THERE'S NO PLACE LIKE HOME

a year in foreclosure

THERE'S NO PLACE LIKE HOME

JOHNNY LEONARD FORD
EDITOR JACKSON KERR

PALMETTO
PUBLISHING

Charleston, SC
www.PalmettoPublishing.com

There's no place like home.
Editor Jackson Kerr

First Edition

Paperback ISBN: 9798822921955

TABLE OF CONTENTS

FORWARD

Over the past few months I have had the chance of meeting with Johnny to talk about his experiences through a difficult time in his life. From what he has told me, this book came together when he was recovering from a major surgery.

In working to process his emotions and handle the situation he was in, he put together this work talking about a difficult time he went through. His style is prompt and from my understanding after working on it, this work is an exploration of that time in his life.

I've been fortunate to have the chance to talk with Johnny about this, and I hope that you find this work as inspiring as I have.

– Jackson Kerr, Editor

INTRODUCTION

This book was literally, well, in as far as years it was fifthteen years in the making, but the thought of it was established back in 2018 after I was recovering from brain surgery. I found out I had a tumor in my left ear canal called an acoustic neuroma that was pressing against my brain, so I had brain surgery at the University of Michigan. I'm so thankful that everything came out Great.

But during my recovery time I decided that after going through a dramatic surgery like that, maybe talking about an ordeal I overcame that gave me strength would help to sharpen my mind again. So I decided to slowly start writing a book. I'd never done anything like this before, but I had a lot of time on my hands, trying to get healthy and get back to work. It was about four months, doing my therapy, sitting down at a computer, and coming up with chapters about everything that happened to my family back in 2010.

It was hard for me, all of this journey came about when I went to the Michigan State Police Training Academy. This was where the Department of Natural Resources Park Ranger Law Enforcement Academy was held. To graduate from the academy you had to pass all classroom required testing, survival tactics training, and participate in daily physical fitness training. Combining all of this with incredible courage and determination to just get through it, period. Some people didn't get through it, some people didn't pass, some people lost their jobs. My biggest fear was that my home would be gone and I wouldn't have a job to come back to after all of this.

For now I just want to share these experiences, to uplift people – when things get tough you just gotta pray about it, knowing there's a light at the end of the tunnel. I think that is so important. I believed that my whole life has been about that, just being an encouragement to others, being humble, praying all the time, and thanking the Lord for the things that you are blessed to have. That's important too.

– Johnny Ford, Author

Chapter 1

MY DAY OFF

On January 19, 2010, I made a call to my wife Jeanne

"Hey honey," I said, "You're not going to believe this. I just lost my job."

Jeanne was silent over her cell phone. She didn't say a word for a few seconds. I realized that in her heart she was scared and worried. Only three days earlier, she had lost her job. Now we were two people with no way to make an income.

"How will we pay our bills and keep our home?"

It felt like yesterday when I uttered those words out of my own mouth. On that day, 6:30 PM on a Thursday night, it was my day off. Looking back at that moment in time changed our lives as we knew it. I was working as a bartender and was let go for having only sixty dollars in the register. It wasn't bad for having only five to eight people in the bar that day. My manager told me that it was the lowest total ever rung up on the day shift. I thought that was strange to hear because a former employee I know told me she had worked several days with forty dollars or less left in the register.

After looking back on the events which followed, I decided that I had been set up. I was the fall guy. The accused. The thief.

It has taken me a while to get over this, maybe I'm not yet because I know that I am not a thief. Someone needed to be blamed and I was the new guy so it was easy to blame me. But they didn't know me yet. They don't know the work ethic that I have and the integrity that I hold dear.

Fact of the matter is, somewhere down the line the owner of the business probably found out who the real thief was. I'm not sure though, the day that I came in to plead for my job, it was obvious that the owners' mind had already been made up because of what his manager had told him. He was there only to cover himself. I decided to take the high road, not to drop dime, or throw any other employee under the bus. When the owner asked me about the low amount in the register and the theft in the building, I told him he would find out soon enough about who the real thieves were.

The day I lost my job, I closed my cash drawer at the end of the shift. There was an employee that was always running late, and that particular day, I earned another thirty-five dollars for the bar which went into the drawer of the employee who was late for work. That extra money would have made my cash drawer total almost one hundred dollars. That isn't bad for five to eight people in the bar all day. That is the truth!

Ask yourself now, should I have lost my job on my day off?

Chapter 2

IT'S PAID FOR, ROAD TRIP OR NOT

What do we do? Stay home or go? We had no way to get a refund or our money back. Jeanne and I had to make that decision. Six months earlier we were doing very well financially, having cookouts, pool and graduation parties at our home. I even sold my Sweet 2001 Red Mustang to pay off our debt and to pay for our trip to Key West. So during our current condition we still had some money in the bank, but no jobs. I decided to go down to the DHS building to get a food card and assistance so that we could have food to eat. I see now that this became a humbling experience for me. I didn't care who saw me or what people thought of me. I had only one focus at this time – making sure that Jeanne, our dog Jada, and I all had food to eat.

After receiving our food card, my next responsibility was to find odd jobs to make money to pay our bills, keep the lights on, and pay our mortgage. These jobs included clearing brush in fields, building decks, painting homes, and picking up bottles and cans to turn in. I did whatever it took to keep our home afloat and to assure Jeanne that everything would be all right.

But deep down I just wanted to feel whole and worthy again, as a man. Many days I felt like a failure. Three weeks before our decision to go on the trip to Florida, I finished the maintenance on our Ford Explorer so that we could drive down to Florida. It would be a 27-hour drive for us because we couldn't afford to fly.

I continued to look for a job and a couple of days later I got a call from a local hotel with a bar in the area. They liked my experience in bartending and customer service, so they hired me. But the only problem was that they would not start me until the end of February. At least I had a job now.

Chapter 3

ON TO KEY WEST; ROAD TRIP

I wasn't sure why the owner of the bar wouldn't start me in early February. I was ready to work. So we finally made up our minds to go to Key West, Florida. We really needed this vacation to give us Some hope and encouragement. We needed to know that life would get better for us.

Many people would probably have doubted our decision, but those people were nowhere to be found in our time of need. We had consistently given to people, anyone who needed some help. Unfortunately we heard nothing but crickets when we needed help. Sometimes that's how it goes. It was time to move on. Now we had to get our taxes done, organize with our friends who were meeting us there, and find a place for our dog to stay while we took this trip. Planning this is where all my organizing skills would evolve.

First we contacted our friend Frank. He would travel with us to Florida and help set the date to depart. We decided on February

11, 2010. Once we departed, our first pit stop was to drop our dog Jada off in Indianapolis, IN where Jeanne's sister Jennifer lived.

Having a place for our dog to stay kept our stress level down. Our next stop was Atlanta, GA. While passing through states like Kentucky and Tennessee en-route to Atlanta, Jeanne and Frank decided to make fun of me. They focused on the fact that I made a large centerpiece for our dining area where our friends would meet at the Mermaid Inn, Key West, Florida.

Ha-ha, very funny you two.

The trip has gone well so far. The Explorer got the best gas mileage I had ever seen, over 530 miles on a tank of gas, which was awesome. Frank paid for all the gas to get us to Florida. He blessed us with that. Thank you Frank.

After twelve hours of travel we finally made it to Atlanta where my sister Elizabeth lives with her family. This is where we stayed to get some good home cooking and a good night's sleep. Thank you baby sister.

The next day was February 12, 2010 and we were ready to head to Florida. However, I had something which was very important for me to do. Three years ago my mother Susie Ford Walker passed away, and this would be our first time visiting her gravesite, since she was buried in Atlanta, GA. As we arrived at the cemetery, I wasn't sure how I would react that day. I just wanted to tell my mother that we were O.K. and not to worry about us.

I became emotional and cried because my mother always worried about her baby boy. I didn't want her to know how bad things had become. But she already knew. I heard her voice tell me "everything will be alright, son." I miss you mom.

Florida, here we come.

The next stop was to see the mother of my best friend Scott in Leesburg, Florida. We also made plans to stop in Orlando to see my friend Bree. While traveling to Leesburg, we stopped to fill up the gas tank again. At this time I told Jeanne I was going to see if our tax money had been deposited in our bank account. Remember that we had limited money and were hoping that our prayers would be answered.

It was there. I felt like leaping for joy. We now had money for our trip and to pay our bills and mortgage. Thank you Jesus. My attitude changed, I felt a fire burning within me. My mother told me not to worry. Once we made it to the house of Scott's mother, we had dinner at the Honeysuckles restaurant. Then we made our way to Orlando to stay the night at my friend Bree's house, as we were exhausted from driving. Bree took very good care of us. We slept like rocks, sorry for snoring, Girl. The next morning we got up, ready to finish our trip and reach our destination. On to Key West.

Chapter 4
KEY WEST: WE'RE HERE

Traveling through Florida was awesome. The landscape was incredible but unfortunately the traffic and Jeanne's yelling at me almost caused me to get out of the vehicle and walk to Key West.

All joking aside, it was an intense ride going through Miami and over the Atlantic Ocean. It felt like we were on a roller coaster. It was very high off the water. We made it to our destination Key West around 3 PM. We're here. Jeanne, Frank, and I were so happy to be here that we tried to put in an early arrival request at our cottage called the Mermaid Cove. It was occupied.

So we had to rent a loft that night. It was really nice. Time to relax now. The loft even had a hot sub which took care of all our aches and pains from the long road trip. Thank you Lord for getting us here safe, sweet dreams.

The next day I woke up very early. It was Valentine's Day, February 14, 2010, the day our vacation officially started. I took a long walk on Duval Street to get the lay of the land again. Five years ago Jeanne and I were here for three days, but so much time had passed that everything had changed. I found myself checking out our rental. It was very cool, five cottages with a courtyard in the middle. Perfect for my centerpiece.

I couldn't wait to go back and tell Frank and Jeanne that our rental was ready for us to arrive. They were really impressed. Once we unpacked I had to go to the airport to pick up our friends who were joining us on this fantastic trip.

I decided to make a sign like limo drivers use so their customers can find them. So I made up a sign which said:

Key West Crew Welcome!

So that when Scott, Susie, Tracy and Laura departed from the plane they could see me. I was amazed at how huge the plane was when it landed. It was bigger than the landing strip. I waited in the airport for my friends to get their luggage. They didn't see me, but they saw the sign which I held above my head. When my friends finally spotted me we all laughed. It was an awesome moment.

Everyone got here safely. Once everyone got all their luggage, we headed over to the Mermaid Cove to check out the living arrangement, unwind and relax. This gave Jeanne another opportunity to laugh with everyone about my centerpiece.

Later that day I felt excited because I set up a Valentine sunset cruise on a ship called the *Apple Dore*. This would highlight the start of the week on the ocean eating food and drinking a lot of cocktails. We couldn't wait to go again because five years ago Jeanne and I went twice on the ship. The only difference was that it was 85 degrees the last time, and this time the temperature was 65 degrees. Still, we had an awesome time with our friends, it was a lot of fun.

Throughout the week we spent many hours in all of the famous bars and restaurants like Maragetville, Captain Tony's, A&B Lobster House, Sloppy Joes, Hogs Breath and Rick's. Many nights we shut those places down at the last call. Many activities took up our time during the week. Jeanne, Laura, Frank, Scott, and Susie went parasailing. There was no way I was going to dangle my feet in the ocean. There are sharks out there, people.

So Tracy and I stayed on land and went sightseeing. We came to this event called Rock Star Karaoke. I couldn't wait to tell the rest of the crew about it. Frank was a very good singer. I was average, but I could sing "Sweet Home Alabama" very well. So the night in question we all ended up at the bar ready to sing.

Lo and behold there was a house band which played the song for a while on stage. Frank proceeded with his usual "Sitting on the Dock of the Bay". He rocked it. When my time came to come up I was ready to kill it. The band kicked in and I was ready. "Sweet Home Alabama" blasted and I started singing. It was awesome.

That was my fifteen minutes of fame, with a standing ovation. I even had a lady ask me when my next set was. She thought I was the lead singer of the band. So cool. We have the whole show on video. As the weekend loomed near, we went dancing, took haunted house tours, visited more bars and more restaurants. During our last couple of days, as we got tired of walking three miles down Duval street, we decided to rent scooters and drive them to all the other events. It was a lot of fun.

So after all of that fun in Key West our trip was coming to an end. We decided to have steaks for dinner on our last night.

I was in charge of being the grill master. I didn't mess any steaks up. Success. Thank you Lord for an incredible vacation with our friends. This was truly awesome. Now it was time to get some rest, we have a road trip in the morning.

Chapter 5

GOING HOME: TIME TO GET TO WORK

As I woke the next morning we had breakfast and I started reflecting on the incredible vacation, a truly great experience. We ate breakfast in the courtyard. I got one opportunity to rave about my centerpiece, everyone still made fun of me for the last time. Our friends' plane was scheduled for departure in the afternoon that day. Jeanne, Frank and I decided to leave for home around noon.

After giving everyone hugs we started our journey home. Key West, Florida to Benton Harbor, Michigan, a trip of twenty-seven hours and over 1,600 miles. I started out the road trip and drove for about ten hours straight. Then Jeanne took over and drove about six hours. I believe Frank drove for four hours. I slept most of those hours while they drove. Now it was time for me to take us to the home stretch. Nashville, TN to Benton Harbor. Once we got to the city limits I was happy that the Lord had watched over us and kept us safe in our travels. Twenty-seven hours of continuous driving. Wow.

Someone asked many years later if I would ever drive that trip again. I replied *No*.

After a couple days of rest and recovery I started my job at the hotel bar. I had a little bit of anxiety in me because now it was back to reality and I couldn't wrap my head around why this new employer wouldn't start me before our vacation. Also the fact that I worked for this company before and it hadn't ended well.

I couldn't trust them, they did not have integrity. But now they are under new management. Let's hope that it works. I had so much fun getting the bar set up and ready for success. It felt good, as I was working again and making money. So I decided to kick up some business by asking a lot of my friends to come out and visit me at the bar on my Birthday because I wanted to work and it would be a great opportunity for the bar sales and to put money in my pocket.

The place was packed with my friends. Wow. I had at least thirty to forty friends on my side of the bar. I worked my tail off taking care of everyone, and they tipped me very well. The other two bartenders who worked with me that night didn't do much work, they sat around and expected me to give them tips that I made. I said NO, not a chance.

Once the night was over I had a very good night in tips; my family and friends really took care of me, now I was on a fast track to paying our mortgage. I decided to give the other bartenders some cash to help them out, but I was not in the business of giving my tips to others who didn't work. I wanted to keep my money. This was the reason why that anxiety kept creeping in, because it was only a week working, putting sales in the register, making money for the business, and still having this feeling that bad things were coming. I couldn't trust the people here; they had a shady tendency.

Three weeks went by and I felt everything was going very well. I was making money, bills were paid and I was feeling great about winning again. My next big shift was on Saint Patrick's Day, March 17, 2010. On this day I was getting ready for a big night, so I went in early to get the bar ready for success. I noticed as soon as I entered the door there was a lady working on my side of the bar. I asked the manager what was going on. He mumbled a response. I asked him once again what was going on. He responded to me that he wanted to bring his sister in. This lady didn't even know how to make a bloody mary. Once again I found myself in a terrible situation working at a bar with shady people.

After I calmed down and regained my composure, I asked for my final check. This was the final straw. Never again would I allow people to treat me this way. Dishonor me , disrespect me, and hurt me again.

I got my final check that night, $250.00. This was all the money I had. I was broke again, how would I pay our mortgage now? Once again, I found myself saying the same words. *Jeanne, you're not going to believe what happened.*

Chapter 6
I GO TO WORK

Am I a bad person, God? Why do these bad things happen to me? I go to work and do my best every day. What's wrong?

I started asking myself these ridiculous questions because of the doubt that was setting in. I started to disbelieve again. *Just stop it, Johnny. I mean it. Stop it.* That's what I told myself subconsciously. A battle raged inside my head and I needed my soul back, I needed my spirit back, I needed to feel well about myself again, just like I did when I went back to the gym in November 2009 around Thanksgiving time. That's right, you heard me, during the holidays.

With no money to spare, my friend Orlando paid for my first three month membership. I was three hundred pounds. That's right, three hundred pounds when I started. Every day the routine was upper body, lower body, then cardio three times a week. I needed to go all out because I was in the biggest loser status.

I was not only pushed by my friends like Orlando, Chad, Tom and Reverend Kenny, everyone in the gym encouraged me. It was awesome. It helped me to lose forty pounds by the time we went on vacation. That's why I was ready for a new start in bartending again. But it didn't last. I knew at this time I had to get my desire back and hold myself accountable. I wouldn't take direction from those who had an agenda to hurt me. You folks can find another sucker – not me.

Never again. My journey for the rest of my life is to win for Jeanne and I. With winning I had to start over with some humility. I had to go down to DHS to get a food card so that we could eat. I loved bartending, but I didn't work for honest people. Putting pride aside, I had to get a career. What could I do that would make me feel whole again and make me feel good about myself?

After praying about what to do, a big light bulb came to me.

I screamed to Jeanne,

"Hey honey, I'm going to interview for a park rangers job for the State of Michigan."

She said "Wow!" This time, with joy.

I said "Wow! I've got to get ready."

I felt it was time to go back to my roots. This was a job I had back in my twenties. I really enjoyed it. The time was now, this was it: I needed this opportunity right now!

When the day came for the interview I was so nervous, but ready to do my best. All the money I had was in my pocket – fifty-three cents. I dressed in black dress pants, black shoes, white shirt and a blue tie. *Here we go.*

I walked into the office and spoke.

"Hello, my name is Johnny Ford. I'm here for the park ranger interview."

The three officers asked me a couple of questions.

"Why do you want to work here?"

I replied, "I just want to work at a place where I can be all that I can be." I thought that sounded good.

"Why are you the best person for the job?"

"There's no one that will work harder than me, sir." After a moment I said "I don't even work here, but if you give me a shot I will out-work everyone in this whole park."

The officers looked at me. "Really?"

"Yes sir. I will show you if you give me this opportunity."

The interview went well. I told the officers "Thank you for your time."

Once I got into my car I said "Please God, I need this."

Chapter 7

A KNOCK AT THE DOOR

The first time I heard that knocking sound it put chills down my spine. It still does. *Bang-bang-bang*; a fist pounding the door like a raid on a home would sound like.

So I opened the door. It was a Berrien County Sheriff delivering me a foreclosure notice from the court; to vacate your home at the end of the month . Most of the time these notices were to vacate in five days.

The first time these notices came were in November of 2009 from the mortgage company representatives. They would sit outside the house and take pictures and then come knock on your door to tell you that your payment was due. I would reply to them by saying "I know that sir" (or miss) and we paid the balance and were caught up with you. But they didn't care, they were just hired hands paid to harass people in desperate need.

The Police were never mean to us. Not only did they deliver foreclosure papers they also included debts which made it to court which were not getting paid. All of this created insurmountable amounts of stress which seemed sometimes too great to overcome. These knocks continued for an entire year.

Your economic status didn't matter. Many families of all walks of life were devastated by the foreclosure crisis.

Chapter 8
CLEARING BRUSH
IN A FIELD

Almost two months had gone by. I was still waiting for a call from the DNR to see if I got the job or not. Knocks on our door continued every week. Jeanne had started to work now and I was doing spring cleaning jobs because the weather just broke from cold to a bit warmer in April.

My first job was clearing brush to put up a pole barn in a field. A guy named Andy, lived half a block away from us hired me. He owned a construction company. Whatever it took, I was ready – I needed to make money. I started out by cutting down trees, then digging up stumps.

This work was extremely hard. I had cuts and bruises all over my body, but I didn't care, I called it a workout and my body healed quickly. After that project was done, I started painting a house near a golf course in Benton Harbor. Many years later, I can still remember the paint color was yellow because all of my clothes were covered in it.

Halfway into completing the house painting, I was up on a ladder, painting the backside of the house when I received a call from our second mortgage company, Fifth-Third Bank. They asked me the same questions like all the other debtors.

"Why haven't you paid your monthly payment?"

I told the lady over the phone that I'm in hardship, broke, and that I don't have a job right now. After that response came out my mouth, I turned around, sat on the ladder, and spoke again.

"I don't want to lose my home. What can you do to help me?"

She must have heard the fear in my voice. She replied,

"Since you have been a loyal customer for five years, how about we lower your monthly payment and remove all the late charges. Would that help you Mr. Ford?"

"Yes." I replied. I couldn't believe this was happening. We just negotiated keeping my second mortgage payment while I was sitting on the back of a ladder, painting a house!

At the end of the work day, my eyes kept focusing on a log cabin home across the street from where I was working. Every day I would see a lady who I did not know. I would say hi to her and she would say hi to me. This happened every day I worked there.

I knew I was a stranger in the neighborhood, but I truly believed because she saw me working hard every day she knew I was a good person. On my last day wrapping up the paint project, I decided to go over to this amazing home and introduce myself to this lady. You would never believe in a hundred years what happened next.

I knocked on her door gently, as I didn't want her to hear the loud knocking which I was accustomed to at my house. She came to the door. When she opened it, I spoke.

"Hi, my name is Johnny Ford and I have been admiring your beautiful home all week."

She said, "Well come on in and take a look at it!"

My mouth dropped to the floor. I could not believe what was happening. This lady was welcoming me into her home, even with me covered in yellow paint all over my body, looking like crap. All I could think of was that God knew I am worthy in His presence.

This home was awesome. The woman showed me around her beautiful home, the fireplace stood two stories high. It had the biggest windows that I have ever seen, with curtains completely open. This is without saying that the whole house was a log cabin. As this incredible tour wrapped up, I looked over and noticed a picture of some grand-kids. As I got closer to see them. I noticed that the pictures were of my friends, James G and Tracy's kids. I stood in their Grandmother's house.

I was blown away. I told the lady "I know your family."

She gave me one of the biggest hugs I had ever received.

Wow.

What a great experience. After I left that home I cried on my way home and asked God to help me keep mine.

Chapter 9
PRIVATE LINE

The knocks kept coming. Papers arrived again and again from the courts. I really needed an answer from the State of Michigan on the Park Rangers job. Later, I heard over the news that the state was going through a hiring freeze and union battles. That is not what I wanted to hear, a hiring freeze. *I need a job right now.*

Well, I had to go back to the drawing board. My friend Andy had a job to build a deck in South Bend, IN. Now I had to drive 40 minutes to work. I didn't even have money for gas, but I accepted the job. This forced me to start picking up bottles again which became a weekly recurring event in my life. Building the deck was awesome. I had learned so many things about carpentry, how to build forms, and squaring the foundation for pouring cement.

So, the next phase of the project was held up due to rain. Even though we stopped working for that week, Andy was always good at paying me for the work I did do. I appreciated that very much. He knew from the beginning that Jeanne and I were going through financial hardship so he took care of us. Thanks, Andy. Well, I went back home for the weekend cutting grass and picking up bottles in the neighborhood.

Once I got enough bottles to cash in, I decided to hang out at Texas Corral before going over to Wings Etc. to watch baseball, basketball, and see some friends. I did this sometimes just to get away from all of the despair I was going through.

This one day in particular, I was really praying for something good to happen to me. Almost like clockwork I got a call on my cell phone. The caller was registered as a private line. I went outside to answer it, and heard this.

"Hello, this is Park Supervisor Montgomery from Warren Dunes State Park. Is this Johnny Ford?"

I replied, "Yes it is sir."

The Park Supervisor spoke again. "*You* have been selected as a finalist for the park ranger's job. Do you accept the position?"

"Yes sir," I replied, "I accept the position."

From there, I was told to go to the park the following week to finish paperwork. Once I hung up my cell phone, I jumped up in the air and said 'Thank you Jesus! I finally have a job.' God is so good.

Chapter 10

BEAST MODE MAN

The next day I called up Andy to tell him that I got the Park Rangers job and that I would not be able to finish his deck. I told him that I was grateful for all the jobs he gave me to earn money to pay bills. He was happy for Jeanne and I.

My first day of work started two weeks before the Memorial Day weekend. When I showed up to work it was back to the drawing board. See, I might be one of the only people in the state who had work for the DNR during the 80's and 90's. I left the department in 1993. When I interviewed for them again in the early 2000's . I did not get hired. But I got a second chance to start a career again in 2010.

Never give up on your dreams; anything is possible. On my first day on the job I started working with the maintenance crew, picking up garbage on the beach. This was very hard work, but I didn't care. I was ready to put my money where my mouth was. Remember, I said that I would out-work anybody in the park? I truly meant it – that was beast mode man. I was determined that I would show my bosses that they made the best hire ever. I never feared the hard work, this was me winning and on a team again.

Many of the crew members were asking me how old I was. I told them I was forty-five years old.

"What?!" they replied.

Age is just a number. These young crew members had no idea what I had to endure. Yeah, I'm a Park Ranger. I have status in many people's eyes, but I stayed humble. Who cares about status when your home is in foreclosure? Who cares about status when you have to go to the DHS building to get a food card so that your family can eat? Who cares about status when you just got hired for the second time for the greatest career ever! But you're still broke and you don't have any money to get to work. So you pick up cans and bottles to put gas in your tank.

Again, who cares about status?

My journey to become a Park Ranger is more important than any status that I would *ever* have.

Chapter 11

SUMMER TIME

Jeanne and I started the summer making a decent income for the first time in six months. She was now working as a manager for Quiznos. She really enjoyed her job so things were going well. Now we had money to get caught up on our mortgage, but the bank still wouldn't take our checks.

Are you kidding me? I thought. *Come on, we can pay it up.*

I found out that once your home is in foreclosure, they don't want your money in payment. What they really want is for you to pay off the total amount borrowed. Which included continuous paper work and home sales in which you have five days to vacate.

We decided that the issue overpowered us and that we needed help. So we contacted a lady named Katie from the Southwest Michigan Neighborhood Housing Services. This organization helped home-owners who wanted to keep their homes from foreclosure. The day we had a meeting with her I brought in all the paperwork that I had.

When she saw all of the papers on home sales, she couldn't believe that we had not been kicked out of our home. I couldn't take the thought of losing our home which we worked so hard on for years. It was not an option.

We stood ready for the battle of our lives. Katie instructed us to get all of our financial information together, including wages, auto loans, car insurance, medical bills, fixed bills, utility charges, bank statements, debt, taxes, and our mortgage papers. Her office faxed all of this information to debtors every week for months. I guess they wanted to ensure that we maintained a job and paid our bills.

Summertime took on a whole new meaning because the heat was turning up. We had to decide if we were going to have our Annual Memorial Day White party. A White Party meant fun, food, drinks, playtime, and dressing up in white like we were going to the beach. Our back yard did have a beach.

Many years, Jeanne and I spent a lot of money on our end paying for everything concerning this event. I worked the day of the party, so Jeanne, Frank, and a few other friends helped to get the fun started. That day was hot, but rain came through the area. By the time I got home the rain had stopped and the party continued. Our back yard was packed full of people who had been coming over for years, enjoying our hospitality.

I had an idea to help us with the cost of this event. I asked Frank, who traveled to Key West with us, to pass a baseball cap around to collect donations. To my surprise, only one person gave us five dollars. I was devastated, upset, furious. We couldn't believe that after all of these years of hosting this awesome event that a crowd of more than fifty people couldn't offer us any help with a donation to help with the cost of food and drinks – not to mention opening up the pool which costs a lot of money every year to run.

That night, after the party was over, I sat down with Jeanne, Frank, Scott, Micheal and a few other friends.

"God is my witness," I said, "I will never host this White party ever again."

That was eight years ago. My philosophy has always been to be a giver, not a taker. But in our time when we needed receiving, giving, and grace, that didn't happen, which had hurt my soul to the core. I knew that in God's eyes we were worthy of that because we always gave. Now, back to reality. The Fords vs Foreclosure.

One of the greatest gifts in life. Is believing in yourself that you can overcome any challenge. Our journey was worth it.

Chapter 12

TROTT & TROTT VS. THE BANK OF AMERICA

The heat was still on. This became the battle of our lives, smacking us in the face everyday. As our mortgage company, Bank of America pushed papers through for foreclosure, as this debt company Trott & Trott took over. They tried to use a back-door approach by issuing us a certified letter to pay in full, rather than giving us a re-modification program to keep our home.

This undermined their efforts because each month we were barely paying our monthly payments, though we did get the payment in on time. But they were demanding over $93,000. Yeah, that's right. They gave us totally different information at the beginning of May, when both parties met to resolve a plan for us to have a fighting chance to keep our home.

I knew this was fishy because a representative from Trott & Trott asked me a question on the phone one day, a couple of weeks later.

"Mr. Ford," he asked, "which company would you like to use, them or us?"

I knew right away that they were playing games with us. We said we would take our changes with our mortgage company, Bank of America. So hit the road Trott & Trott. Back to the drawing board. We continued gathering all our cost-of-living information. Now we concentrated on our bank statements going back three years in case an audit happened.

Katie informed us that this was used to check patterns of spending. So I retrieved all the bank statements going back three years. This information collected brought back some very hard memories for me.

Three years before this, in the 2008 stock market crash, I stepped in and out of jobs because bar owners couldn't pay their staff. This is when we started drinking almost every day. We had a lot of time on our hands. I usually worked one weekday, then the weekend. So we used the other days for more drinking. Our alcohol of choice was Tall Boys and cheap. I thought if they had to check our bank statement, if they audited us, they would see Angelo's food.

We did go there to get some food. But this place was masquerading as a liquor store. We would buy natural light twenty-two ounce 15-pack and finish it off every day. Drinking, drinking and drinking some more. This is the way we coped with despair and hardship. I would never say I was an alcoholic. Many years in the past I modeled and won bodybuilding contests for beer companies where social drinking took place all the time.

But that's what it was. Now we were at home drinking every night. A few years later, Jeanne got very sick. It scared the life out of me because I didn't know if she was going to live. That day, with her in the hospital, I took a vow that I would never drink any alcohol of any type ever again from that day forward. Now, eight and a half years later, Jeanne and I are alcohol-free and healthy. Thank you Jesus.

Chapter 13
BOSS MAN

The summer time has now come to an end. The State Park was just as busy as I remembered it in the 80's and 90's. One day, at the end of August. Park manager Terrell, called me over the radio to report to his office ASAP. As I walked to his office, I kept asking myself what I had done. I got to work on time every day, and worked hard. What could this meeting possibly be about?

As I approached Mr. Terrell's office door, he spoke.

"Come on in Ford."

He had a habit of calling everyone by their last names. As a former U.S. Marine, with a deep voice, that was how he would recognize you.

"Have a seat," he said.

"Yes sir, Boss Man." I called him Boss-Man because he was a Boss in my eyes.

Mr. Terrell started asking me how my first summer was at the park and whether I enjoyed working here.

"Yes sir, Boss-Man." I said.

The next words out of his mouth changed the scope of how I felt about myself and my life forever. See, I had always had strong men in my life; my dad, uncles, cousins, teachers, and coaches as role-models.

Boss-Man said to me, "Ford, I made a mistake in 2006. I should have hired you back then. Maybe this could have changed all the hardship in your life which I believe you have gone through."

I didn't speak, but asked myself how he knew about that.

He spoke again to me. "I know when a man has a purpose to work hard, be a leader, and provide for his family. I see all of that in you Ford."

The next thing that the Boss-Man said rocked my world.

"By the way, Ford, you're one the best rangers I have ever hired!"

With shock on my face, I said "Thank you sir." and left his office to go home. In my car I started crying and I couldn't stop. I sat alone in my car. Suddenly I heard a voice. I believe it was God speaking to me.

"Get up and follow me."

Once I got home from this incredible experience, I spoke to Jeanne.

"Come on. We got a lot more work to do."

Chapter 14

HEY, IT'S FOOTBALL SEASON

As I mentioned earlier, we had a lot of work to do. Autumn had arrived. Labor Day had just passed. Now the end of September is approaching and I will be getting laid off soon. That's right, laid off. I forgot to tell you that earlier. Once you're hired as a Park Ranger, you have to work your way up the seniority line to gain more working hours.

Well, I was back to odd jobs and picking up cans. But this time around I was able to get a security job checking I.D.s at a night-club. This really helped keep the bills paid, and the cable on. At least I could watch football which kept my competitive fire going.

Unfortunately, the bad news started up again. Those knocks at the door. I called it the fall knock-off. *Here we go again.* Just as I thought they were over.

We received that rude awakening to let us know who was in charge. Back to calling the mortgage company. Almost every day I found myself telling someone that I wanted to keep my home.

I must have said that a thousand times this past year. That's all I wanted to do.

The gut punch came in October, a letter in the mail with the words -

Notice of Intent to Accelerate Payment

The words on that paper meant a home sale notice. The charge on the paper read $20,290.

Wow.

We didn't have that kind of money.

No one in our family had this amount of money. I started to ask myself what are we going to do now. Everything around the house became calm and quiet. I was not sure what was going on, but something came over me.

Something had happened two days earlier, before the notice to accelerate payment came. I didn't want to believe it, but I thought I heard God speak to me for the second time.. I had never had this happen to me before, I'm listening.. This voice was otherworldly, out of this world; subtle, but stern.

God spoke to me and said *Follow me, follow me.*

But it soon became clear to me, my interpretation of it was *Follow up!*

Chapter 15
FOLLOW UP

When God spoke to me, He said *Follow me*. 'Follow up' became the catalyst which I used when I called Bank of America. At this time I was on a mission which I hoped would define my life going into the new year. Christmas time had come, Jeanne and I still put the Christmas tree up and decorated the house not knowing if this would be the last year of it.

The first phase of my mission was to call anyone who could help us. We got tired of all the run-around. They wouldn't take our money. They kept putting us on hold with the same excuse-they couldn't find our paperwork. So to all the people working at our mortgage company who did not truly care about Johnny and Jeanne Ford, shame on you.

The good news is that one person truly did care about us. Her name was D. Gregg. Mrs. Gregg is a true champion in her field for helping families through foreclosure. Her only focus in our situation was to keep all of our paperwork at the top of the list and not the bottom. I informed her that we continue to receive many knocks at the door which would not stop.

Why was this happening all the time?

Why wouldn't they take payments from us?

Why were there home sales on Monday, telling us that we must be out of our house by Friday? I explained to Mrs. Gregg that these house calls caused people to give up. People are scared by these calls and they lose hope. That is why 97% quit and 3% might make it to the end of this nightmare. I told Mrs. Gregg that I wasn't certain what our outcome would be, because I wanted to keep our home.

Chapter 16
HARDSHIP LETTER

The knocks continued into the new year of 2011. January was cold that year, but we managed to keep the bills and utilities paid up. Still, foreclosure papers arrived in the mailbox. One day in particular, in mid-January, another knock sounded at the door. I answered it like I always do and it was the sheriff once again.

He spoke.

"Sir, I have some papers for you."

He handed me another home sale notice.

"I thought that the mortgage company said they would stop." I said under my breath.

The sheriff heard and answered me. "I know what your family is going through. I'm dealing with the same thing."

"What!" I said.

"Yeah, my home is in foreclosure too."

I found the solitary word "Wow" coming out of my mouth. This was the first time I didn't feel totally alone during this experience.

After the sheriff left I heard the voice of God speaking to me once again. Now the third time.

Follow me!

I replied "God, what do I have to do?"

At this time all I could think of was the letters we'd received in the mail and the sheriff's notices. I guess God meant that we should write a letter. So we did.

Jeanne and I tilted the letter the 'Explanation of Hardship', addressing this original letter to the mortgage company:

During the months of January 2010, both Jeanne and I, Johnny Ford, had become unemployed. Many continuous months have gone by without any job opportunities which have left us unable to pay our mortgage payments.

Since then we have both been blessed with jobs. My job started in May as a park ranger for the State of Michigan and my wife Jeanne's job as a General Manager at Quiznos Subs.

Our goal is to receive a modification program loan which could help us get back on track. We love our home and want to keep it.

Thank you,
Johnny and Jeanne Ford
1/31/2011

Chapter 17

CONCEALMENT

At the beginning of February a bunch of guys at the gym were talking about buying guns and taking a concealed weapons class. My friend Chad who worked out with us owned a gun shop in town. I became very interested in buying a gun. For some reason I felt that the timing was right to have this responsibility, especially before I left for the DNR Law Academy in a few weeks.

Maybe in the back of my mind I worried about Jeanne's safety at the house because I planned to leave soon to become a DNR Officer. Jeanne would be home by herself handling everything, dealing with the home needs, foreclosure, and possible knocks at the door from creditors. I knew deep down inside that Jeanne could handle it if she ever needed our weapons to protect herself. I felt this way because we both spent some time at the shooting range, and most of the time she shot better than I did.

A lot of men wouldn't say that their wife was a better shot than they were. But it happened and I admitted to it. The good news is that I redeemed myself since then because I shoot more now. My best friend Scott remembered from our Key West trip was worried about me. He thought I had bought guns to ward off anyone trying to take our home.

So I had to spend time calming him down, reassuring him that this wasn't the case and that I wasn't insane. It was just for protection, and I was in the right frame of mind. Well in a few days I was leaving for the academy, so Jeanne and I went out to dinner to celebrate Valentine's Day.

This was a full circle moment, because we had done this same thing a year ago under different circumstances, but still in foreclosure.

Chapter 18
SERGEANT OF ARMS

February 14, 2011 – I started my journey to the Michigan State Police Training Academy. It became very real for me that I had the weight of the world on my shoulders and there was no turning back now. Once I got to the State Police Facility I knew that this structure would be very demanding for anyone trying to reach the next level of success.

This was going to be the hardest thing I ever endured in my life. I kept telling myself *I am going to make* it. I was forty-five years old, and there were two other men, 51 and 52 years old who were with me. 95% of the class was made up of 20-something year-old men and women. I was an old man in a young person's world trying to become a Park and Recreation Officer.

As we entered the hallways, we were summoned to a class room. Once we entered, we were told to drop all our bags and to line up, shortest to tallest. At this time we were taught how to march. All I could think of at this time was that it was going to be a military base academy. Every day you made your bed, marched everywhere, eating, sleeping, having class, and participating in physical training.

Get ready to be broken down again. The thought constantly came to my mind. What else could I endure, including foreclosure of my home?

My first night at the training academy I didn't sleep well. The only thing on my mind was Jeanne. I couldn't imagine the horror that she faced being alone at home, knowing that our home could be taken away from us at any time. I took answering all the knocks at the door, home sell notices, eviction papers and all the financial problems on my shoulder.

I took all the burden to keep it away from Jeanne. Now I wasn't trying to be sneaky. I just didn't want her to feel any of the pain of what we were going through this past year. Now she sat alone at home, dealing with it. We still had so much work to do to keep our home-- now I was away from home.

God, what am I going to do to help protect Jeanne?

The next day we marched to breakfast then to the classroom. The instructors advised us to pick a Sergeant of Arms for the academy. I looked around to see who they were going to pick for their vote. In my mind I hoped that they wouldn't pick me. I had too much on my plate. My home was in foreclosure, I was about to lose everything, I had nothing to give. Now they wanted me to lead men and women. I told myself I wasn't worthy of this.

As the recruiting of the Sergeant of Arms continued, I could feel the glances of Ranger looking my way. I tried to avoid eye contact with them. I kept telling myself that I couldn't do it.

Get up and follow me.

God spoke to me a fourth time. Once again it was loud and clear.

So I stood up in front of my class of fellow Rangers and spoke. "I will do it."

Wow. With that, I became the next Sergeant of Arms.

Chapter 19

MARCHING

Early rise, recruits. The sounds of the wake-up bugle echoed through the camp. It was time for physical training at 5 AM. *Get up Park Rangers, it's time to go.*

As the Sergeant of Arms, I had to make sure that everyone was in line and ready to march everywhere we had to go. This included physical training, classroom, breakfast, lunch, dinner, and study time. I still had doubt in my ability to stay focused and lead my peers through these seven weeks of training.

My mind reeled with turmoil and doubt. I kept asking myself if I could do this. At this point I had no choice. *Lead 'em Johnny, lead 'em.* So I did. No one in the building had a clue what my family was going through. My wife Jeanne sat at home alone, while I kept that stern face. I had to be the man in charge, the leader of the pack, the strong one. I did all of that to show everyone that I had Courage to lead and to show everyone that I was worthy of this position. But deep down my soul was hurting, because I didn't want to lose my home.

How could I explain to Jeanne while at the Academy that she had to get a moving truck, call the few friends that we had at that time, and vacate the house at a moment's notice? That was not an option for me. So I continued to make it, not fake it, because I'm not fake. You tell me how you would handle this when all the odds were stacked against you. Let me tell you, when I said earlier that this was one of the hardest things I had to endure in my life, I wasn't lying. My emotions were so bottled up in me that if the park rangers could have seen my face they could probably tell that something was going on. But I always kept up front, straight ahead with eyes focused. Maybe some of the Michigan State Troopers saw the fear in my soul.

Chapter 20

HOME COOKING

Every morning we filed in line at ten minutes to 5 A.M. I could tell that everyone was tired. I had been staying up studying until 3 A.M. every morning because there was no option for me to fail any test. I had to pass every test to keep my job. We got through our first week of training with flying colors, everyone passed their test. But no one was ready for what the second week would entail.

This was hell week, which also went by the more formal name of Survival Tactics. Requirements included passing classroom examinations at 80% and your particle test at a 100%. Those who didn't were sent home packing with no job. There was a lot at stake for me. I had to pass because I was the leader and people were counting on me to encourage them to win as well.

At the end of the week, I also looked forward to my birthday. I faced incredible pressure. If I passed every test I would get to go home and enjoy my birthday with my wife and friends. If I didn't pass, I would have to go home to my wife and tell her that I didn't make it and that I had lost my job as well. If that had happened we would have no means to fight foreclosure and keep our home. That nightmare still remains.

Fortunately I passed every test.

Afterwards it was time to go home and celebrate. Coming home refreshed me, especially because I believed that I finally had the strength and courage to keep battling to keep our home and my job. Jeanne prepared an awesome birthday for me, for which I was grateful.

It was time to go back to the academy. Every day we had room inspection, bed inspection, physical training, classroom, study time, and of course, marching, marching, and marching.

The academy instructors told me to keep the recruits focused. I did that. When anyone got out of hand I took them to one side and told them to get their act together. They didn't just make themselves look bad, they made the other rangers look bad as well.

One day in particular I was taken out of the classroom and one of the instructors reamed me. She explained to me that one of the other recruits was not walking in a straight line or keeping his eyes ahead. He got caught watching television. Some idiot had put me in a bad situation. I was livid. Well, that's what I had to deal with, being Sergeant of Arms, dealing with personalities. I took care of that problem and it never happened again.

The time came for me to get my ducks in a row. I did very well at the academy under the extreme circumstances I faced. An idea occurred to me after marching the recruits to dinner. I ate quickly, making time for me to run upstairs. Pulling out my cell phone I dialed my mortgage company. At this point I had to negotiate a deal to keep our home. I became relentless. I even stayed in town on the weekend, because I didn't go home much. The State of Michigan provided hotel rooms for recruits that had long travels home to stay the weekends. Sometimes Jeanne come up to visit me when I stayed in town.

We spent many weekends just holding each other and praying. I knew in my heart that she was worried and scared. So was I. I told her that I wasn't giving up. When Jeanne wasn't able to come to Lansing I had the greatest pick-me-up ever to keep me going. I was able to go to my sister Tonya's house because she lived fifteen minutes from the training academy.

This was the time for me to eat some awesome food. The food at the academy was ok, but too high in sodium. Tonya would fix the meals we had during our childhood. Greens, cornbread, mashed potatoes, and pot roast. Wow, it tasted *so* good. I needed that so much; to be around great food and my family.

Chapter 21
GRADUATION DAY

As I mentioned, I was able to spend time with my sister and niece. It was a time filled with laughter and great food. At the end of week six I decided to go over to my sister's house one more time. I wasn't planning on going home this time because I had only six days to achieve my goal of becoming a Park Officer for the Department of Natural Resources. But in the back of my mind I still thought of foreclosure. Whether we would be able to keep our home was uncertain at this point.

My sister Tonya began to set the table with awesome food and once again it was time to eat. As I started plowing into a big plate of food. My cell phone rang. Answering it, I heard Jeanne's voice telling me that we received a letter from the mortgage company. I told her to open it.

Her heart raced and I began to sweat as I waited to hear what the notice said. Would this be the end of our journey? Finally, she spoke and read the letter.

Dear Jeanne and Johnny Ford,

*The B.A.S. Home Loan Servicing L.P., the Bank of America Company that services your loan **has approved you** for a loan modification program to help you achieve more affordable payments to keep your home.*

When I heard the word *approved* I dropped to my knees in front of my sister and niece. I cried and prayed to God.

"Thank you Father, Thank you Father for saving us. I gave you everything I had. Thank you."

We won.

Jeanne, my family and I all cried. I asked Jeanne what the rest of the letter said. She told me that we had five days to get all the important information and foreclosure proceeding papers back to the mortgage company. This fell on the day after my 6-week exam. I rushed home to get to the bank and post office to mail all the information. This was it, I couldn't believe it. We had been blessed to keep our home. That final weekend before graduation was awesome.

Jeanne and I celebrated; we felt as though we had climbed to the top of Mount Rushmore. All the pain, hardship, despair and doubt left our bodies for the first time in well over a year. We had done it.

Now it was week seven, back to the academy. It was time to close the deal. I was on fire that week. I knew that God had tested me to the brink. He told me to follow him and I did. That week marching became the battle cry against any resentment in my heart. I embraced everything because no one knew anything about what was going on in my life. The pain I felt. My goal was to lead the rangers who had elected me Sergeant of Arms. I prayed to God that I wouldn't let them down, and I believe in my heart that I didn't.

This current unit completed their journey. We made it. Now it was time, Graduation Day. This fell on April Fools day, a day of pranks. This started at four o'clock in the morning.

At 4 AM I heard a piece of paper slide under the door. Getting up, I stepped to the door and retrieved the paper, reading it carefully.

Sargent,

You did a great job leading your Rangers through Academy training. There's no physical training today, get some rest.

Yeah right.

I got the rangers up anyway and we worked on our Graduation March before room inspection. We found out later that the letter was legit. April Fools.

Everything seemed so surreal that day at the Michigan State Police Training Academy. This was the place where I learned that I was strong, full of courage to win, and succeed. We began to make our last march as a unit. I made sure everyone was crisp, clean, and that boots were polished. We looked and sounded professional. We looked awesome.

Being able to see my wife Jeanne, my sister Tonya, my friend Frank and all my managers and supervisors who gave me this Incredible opportunity was special. The icing on the cake was when Jeanne pinned my badge onto my uniform. I looked at her.

"We made it." I said.

God, this was the greatest day ever.

For everything that Jeanne and I went through, all I can say is never quit. God has a plan for you, follow him. There's no place like home.

God said follow me. And I did. I became a Michigan State Parks and Recreation Officer. The greatest career in the world.

ACKNOWLEDGEMENTS

Thank you Jennifer and Cydney for watching Jada during our trip

Thank you Frank for paying our way to Florida.

Thank you Elizabeth, for hosting us during our trip.

Thank you Tonya and Gabby for providing excellent food and hosting me during my training.

Thank you Johnny & Jeanne Ford.